Teach your child
SOCCER

John Adams

Former Regional Coach (North) for the Football Association

GW00720391

LEPUS BOOKS

106, HAMPSTEAD ROAD, LONDON NW1 2LS

©1976 by Lepus Books.

An associate company of Henry Kimpton Ltd.
106, Hampstead Road, London NW1 2LS

All rights reserved. No part of this publication may be
reproduced, stored in a retrieval system, or transmitted,
in any form or by any means, electronic, mechanical,
photocopying, recording or otherwise, without the
prior permission of the publishers.

ISBN 0 86019 021 8 (limp)
     0 86019 025 0 (case)

IBM Setting by Print Origination, Orrell Mount,
Hawthorne Road, Bootle, Merseyside L20 6NS

Printed Offset Litho in Great Britain by
Cox & Wyman Ltd, London, Fakenham and Reading

Contents

The parent as teacher and coach

The parent as teacher and coach

Are parents important?

There can be no doubt that the best thing that can happen to any boy who would wish to become a top class soccer player, or a top class performer at any game of activity, come to think of it, is to be born into a family where parents have enthusiasm for the particular game or activity concerned. Indeed it is almost true to say that without parental enthusiasm there is very little chance in Association Football for the boy to reach the top.

This does not mean to say that the parents themselves will, in the case of the father, always have been exceptionally gifted as players. Indeed there are many instances of boys coming from such parentage who learn, not enthusiasm for the game, but exactly the reverse. They perhaps feel early in life that they cannot match the father's prowess and therefore become discouraged. Equally on the other hand there are the cases, Jack Charlton and Bobby Charlton would be cases in point, where the main influence has been that of the mother, who through enthusiasm and love of Association Football has developed an interest in the boy at a very early age.

It is of course possible for parents to carry their own interest and enthusiasm too far, and to push boys into situations which they do not wish to enter. However, there is, in my opinion, absolutely no doubt that properly controlled parental enthusiasm is the key stone to early involvement and probably to subsequent success in any sport.

Boys born into a home where Association Football is part of the tradition, by virtue of the father or mother, or better still, both, being associated with the game in some capacity are indeed fortunate. Parental involvement with the game, albeit from the point of view of playing, coaching, administering, or merely from the largest of all involvements, spectating, can be the springboard to success. There will be very few such parents who have not spent considerable time either in the garden, on the beach, or even on the playing field, enthusing and encouraging their own children from an early age. In this book it is hoped that we shall be able to build upon that enthusiasm, by giving parents who would encourage their children, some basic information and basic practices in which they can involve themselves and their children, secure in the certain knowledge that they are going to improve and develop not only the interest but also the application and attitude of the boy towards the game.

One would go so far as to say at the moment that it is even more important than ever before, that parents take an interest in their child's development as far as Association Football is concerned. The widening of the Physical Education curriculum in schools has led in many cases, to Association Football activities being diminished within the school system. Consequently boys who may wish for more involvement, either at an earlier age or indeed at a later age, may be denied this where previously it was available. Later in the book we shall talk about the organisation of teams and involvement in competition and it is significant to note that many teams are now organised for boys by parents and the like. These teams are filling a need which has been felt for some time due to a decrease in the number of opportunities for boys to play soccer in school.

Are parents important? I would say they are vital, if a boy's full love and potential for the game are to be developed.

How to start

We have already identified enthusiasm as the most vital constituent for any parental involvement with their children in the teaching and playing of the game. However, enthusiasm alone is not sufficient. In terms of Association Football, one of the biggest problems, for those of us who have been involved in developing the pool of coaches which now form the backbone of the Football Association Coaching Scheme, has been to persuade people that because they themselves have a passionate interest and involvement in the game that they do not necessarily know all there is to know about it. And even more than that, that they do not know necessarily the best way to present the game to boys of different ages in order to do the best thing from the point of view of the boy.

Certainly it must be understood from the start that games of eleven a side, as played in professional Football and Senior Football, are not necessarily the best ways to develop skill in young players.

This is a major problem within the school system where schoolmasters will insist on making little boys of even below the age of 11 play in eleven a side football. It is proved beyond doubt that skills are best learnt in smaller situations, especially when the youngsters are not of sufficient maturity to be able to take in the complicated picture that the eleven a side game of Association Football presents.

The parent therefore would do well to think about the game of Association Football and try and decide in his or her own mind what the major constituents of the game are.

What is football?

It will be found that there are two broad areas, (1) Techniques and (2) Skill.

Techniques can be defined if you like as the basic mechanics of the game, for example, kicking, heading, shooting, dribbling, trapping, etc. As techniques they can be practised on their own or alternatively they can be combined with other techniques according to any specific requirement.

Skills have been defined as the application of technique within the game situation. That may sound high-flown, but what in actual fact it means is that skills are developed when everything that is present within the game is to be found. For example in any practice to develop skill, there must be players who will co-operate, that is to say, team-mates. Secondly there must be players who will be opponents and thirdly there must be a direction or a target to be reached in terms of the practice.

A shrewd observer will therefore see that skill practices develop skill and also technique, but technique practices, that is to say, practices performed without opposition and often without supporting players, can only develop technique and not skill.

What therefore should the good parent attempting to improve his child and build enthusiasm do? The answer is plain. He must ensure that the child is involved in both skill and technique work and also that the skill and technique work has an outlet in some form of organised game. The organised game with very young boys, will perhaps be only of three a side or perhaps five a side, certainly it should not extend to eleven a side.

The parent with one child is restricted, in many cases, to practising technique in isolation, but this need not necessarily be a bad thing at an early age. One word of warning however; technique practices on their own not only do not develop skill, but also can become boring and the children can become frustrated. A high premium therefore is put on the inspirational quality of the parent, and also upon his patience and encouragement for the child. The obvious solution to small families is of course for parents to involve themselves in practice with boys from other families. In this way skill practices can be developed and the general enjoyment level raised, while skill is improving.

In this book, therefore, we show simple technique practices which may be practiced in isolation and we also show basic practices for skill which may be developed when larger groups of boys are present. These larger groups may in actual fact only constitute two or three boys, although of course according to space they can be developed to accommodate more. Certainly the average technique practice contained herein may be attempted within the confines of the average garden. Parents with enthusiasm for soccer are known not to resent too much the odd broken window, but obviously it must be stated that the majority of the practices are best developed in the wider confines of some recreational area or playing field.

Let's look at skill

In terms of skill the things that are required of the player are as follows:-
1. To be able to win or gain possession of the ball. This includes aspects of tackling and intercepting.
2. Controlling the ball, this includes all aspects of trapping with various parts of the body and various principles of taking the pace off the ball.
3. Using the ball, this naturally involves all the problems of passing, heading, dribbling and shooting etc.

These indeed are the basic skills of the game. However, the game is not only built up of these, for it is a game of ideas.

These ideas are very closely related to the making of decisions and it must be understood that if success is to be achieved in applying basic skills then it is necessary for the player to understand how to develop ideas. In short, he must have practice in making decisions as to what to do with the ball.

Skill in football has been defined very clearly by one authority as follows. Thinking of the situation as a player receives the ball, he asks himself, 'What does the player have to do?' Can you imagine the situation? There is the player on the field with the ball at his feet. What has to happen for success?

Firstly the player has to decide WHAT TO DO. Secondly he has to decide WHEN TO DO IT. Thirdly he has to decide HOW TO DO IT. These are the basic decisions that all players have to make, and it will be readily seen and agreed that the first two decisions WHAT TO DO and WHEN TO DO IT are the decisions of ideas and timing. These decisions can only be developed by practices involving skill. That is to say, practices with team-mates and opponents present. HOW TO DO IT is a matter of technique and therefore this can be established in practices not involving other players or at least only one player, who will receive the ball.

In Association Football it has been established that in every 90 minutes of play a player may only have the ball for a maximum of something like 3 minutes. For 87 minutes, therefore, he is involved in getting into position to receive the ball or alternatively getting into position to get the ball back from the opposition. However, the 3 minutes that he has the ball are absolutely vital. It is no use players becoming totally successful at getting into position to receive the ball and totally successful in taking up positions to get the ball away from opponents, if, having received the ball or won it back, they immediately part with it to the opposition.

Consequently we should spend time on technique practice, but equally it will be seen that technique practice, by the same token is no use on its own. A player who is excellent on the ball, but totally inefficient off it, can only be effective for a maximum of 3 minutes out of every 90.

In a recent game a midfield player was watched closely and it was found that during the whole game of 90 minutes he touched the ball 40 times. Remember, a midfield player will have as much, if not more, involvement than the majority of his team-mates. This player's total number of contacts came to 40. In other words one touch of the ball, for every two minutes of the game, or thereabouts. Of those 40 contacts he was successful in passing the ball to his own team-mates 18 times. On 22 occasions he gave the ball away to the opposition. Therefore, by any token of success he was only successful, in terms of ball work, on 18 occasions out of 90 minutes. This is patently not up to the standard that the player himself, or indeed anyone else would wish. Players must understand that not only do we require involvement in the game, but when we have the ball, we pass the ball to a person wearing the same coloured shirt as ourselves. This sounds so trite when one says it. Yet when one observes games at the majority of levels, one is often forgiven perhaps for thinking that the players have never heard of this simple philosophy. Parents at the earliest age can start to ensure that their children understand the basis of play by establishing this requirement.

Football is firstly a passing game. A game which involves other techniques and skills. But passing comes first. The parent who would act as a teacher or coach to his own child or the children of others, would do well to keep his enthusiasm in encouraging the development of correct technique allied to good decision making. By using practices for technique, skill and encouraging co-operation between players in small sided games, the parent can make a most valuable contribution to the child's development. These principles will form the basis of our work and in the next section of this book we shall analyse the fundamentals of the game from the point of view of technique and skill and proceed to examine some of the basic concepts of attack and defence which might be taught in small sided games.

"Football is firstly a passing game." David Adams, aged 6, concentrates totally on learning the fundamental skill of the game.

Practice with a purpose

Accurate passing (inside of the foot)

1. Check the non-kicking foot is level with the ball.
2. Check the kicking foot is turned out to bring the inside of the foot in contact with the ball.
3. Check contact is made through the middle of the ball with a firm push THROUGH it.

Practice

A garage door or a wall is a useful thing to have around. Mark an area 4 yds wide and see how many times the ball can be played against the wall through the marked area.

Start the practice 3 yds away and gradually increase the distance. To start with allow the child two touches. One to control the ball and one to play it off. As ability increases reduce the touches to one only.

A good competitive practice can be played by two or more players. One plays the ball and the other has to return it through the marked area and so on.

Accuracy is the first requirement for all passes.

Diagram A

SET A TEST

HOW = Techniques (Diag. A)

Under 12's
From five yards play the ball with one touch through the gap on 5 consecutive occasions.

Under 14's
As above. Extend distance to 9 yards.

Over 14
As above. Extend distance to 12 yards.

WHEN AND WHERE = Skill (Diag. B)

Mark out a small area roughly 10 yards square 01, 02, 03. Try to build passes against an opponent X.

U12's make at least 5 passes. U14's 10 passes. Over 14 Over 20 without the ball passing out of the square or the opponent winning it.

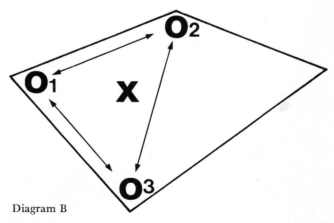

Diagram B

Passing with the outside of the foot

1. Check the non-kicking foot is slightly behind the ball.
2. Check the kicking foot is turned slightly inwards to bring the outside of the foot in contact with the ball.
3. Make contact on the inside of the ball with the outside of the foot and hit through it on the mid-line of the ball.

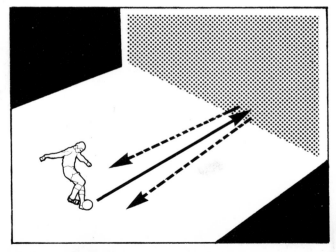

Diagram A

Practice

Using a garage door or wall as with the inside of the foot, stand with a ball at feet 10 yards or so away from the rebound surface.

The ball is played against a wall or door with the outside of the foot and the rebound is replayed in the same way.

An advanced practice can be to start facing the left hand side of the wall and play the ball with the outside of the right foot. The rebound will come back at an angle causing the next rebound to be played further along the wall. Progress until you reach the right hand end of the wall and then retrace your steps by playing the ball with the left foot again using the outside of the foot.

SET A TEST

OUTSIDE OF THE FOOT

HOW = Techniques (Diag. A)

Under 12's
From 5 yards play the ball against the wall with one touch on 5 consecutive occasions.

Under 14's
As above. Extend distance to 9 yards

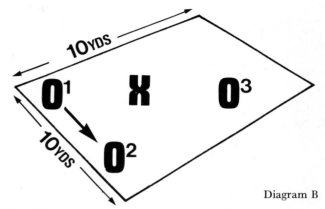

Diagram B

Over 14
As above. Extend distance to 12 yards.

WHEN AND WHERE = Skill (Diag. B)

Mark out a small area roughly 10 yards square. 01, 02 and 03 try to build passes against an opponent X using the outside of the foot. Every outside of the foot pass made counts 1 point and the aim is as follows:

U12's make at least 5 passes. U14's make at least 10 passes. Over 14 make at least 20 passes without the ball passing out of the square or the opponent winning it. Only passes made with the outside of the foot count.

Long high passes

1. Make sure there is a well balanced approach run into the ball. Players should neither overstretch nor produce too short running strides. The aim is to get the non-kicking foot to the side of and a little way behind the ball.
2. The point of contact is for the instep to hit the bottom of the ball. Hitting the bottom of the ball makes the ball rise.
3. Follow through. A follow through is required for distance and should be made in the direction that the pass is required to go.

Practice

Here it is a good idea to try to go onto a football field or if a field is not available to use a length of recreation or garden area of approximately 30 yards.

Using a football pitch have the ball placed on the edge of the centre circle nearest the goal. The task is to hit the ball with a long pass into the goal. A scoring system to add interest and incentive can be produced by awarding 3 points for a ball which goes straight into the goal, 2 points for a ball which bounces in the 6 yard box before entering the goal and 1 point for a ball which goes into the goal having bounced before the penalty area.

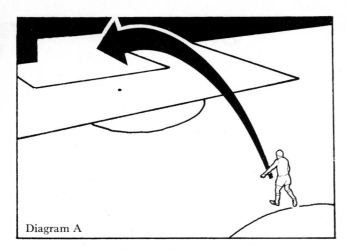

Diagram A

HOW = Techniques (Diag. A)

Under 12's
Play the ball over partner to land in centre circle without a bounce. Score at least twice out of every six attempts.

Under 14's
As above. Reach centre circle at least three times out of every five attempts.

Over 14's
As above. Reach center circle at least four times out of every five attempts.

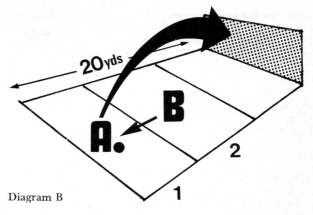

Diagram B

WHEN AND WHERE = Skill (Diag. B)

A stands in an area roughly 10 yards wide. Parent B plays the ball into this area from a position in another area roughly 10 yards wide. B then moves either forward, to threaten A, or back to cut off his pass. A has to play the ball over him to succeed. A wall 10 yards further to the rear of the practice area is a big help.

U12's should aim for 3 out of 5 successes. U14's should aim for 4 out of 5 successes. Over 14's should aim for 5 out of 5 successes. The parent must act as an active opponent to make this a practice for skill. If he does not, it becomes a practice for technique alone.

17

Chipping

1. Check the non-kicking foot is alongside the ball.
2. Check the leg and foot are brought quickly down onto the ball to produce backspin to make the ball rise. A 'stabbing' action is required.
3. Check that the point of impact on the ball is made at the bottom to ensure maximum backspin and therefore maximum rise in the shortest possible time.

Practice

On a football field the player should stand on the penalty spot and try to chip the ball onto or over the bar.

In a back garden or even on the field it is quite possible to have a partner to chip the ball over, as in the diagram opposite. Often the parent will be able to act as the partner and his or her additional height will add impetus to the practice. Again the player should stand approximately 12 yards away and as success is gained he should be allowed to move nearer to the barrier. The nearer to the barrier the more is the requirement for the ball to rise steeply and the greater quality of backspin is required.

HOW = Techniques (Diag. A)

Under 12's
Score 1 point every time the ball is chipped over the top of the partner. To check that a chip and not a lofted pass was made, the ball should check on landing. That is to say it

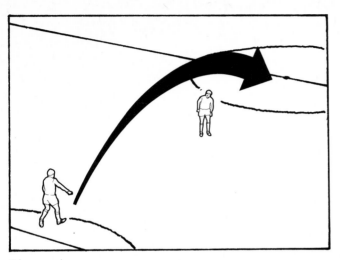

Diagram A

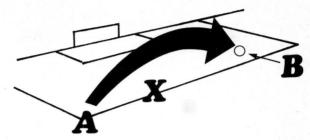

Diagram B

WHEN AND WHERE = Skill (Diag. B)

Parent X plays the ball to the player on the edge of the penalty area. The ball is chipped over the parent to colleague B running in. Colleague B shoots for goal. Score 1 point for every successful chip and a further 2 points when B scores immediately having run on to the ball.

Under 12's should attempt to gain at least 6 points from every 5 attempts. Under 14's should attempt to score at least 10 points from every 5 attempts. Over 14's should go for the maximum of 15 points from every 5 attempts.

should spin slightly backwards rather than travel immediately on.

Under 14's
Score 1 point every time the ball is chipped over the partner and lands in the centre circle.

Over 14's
Players in both under 14 and over 14 age groups should be striving for 5 out of 5 successes.

Volley passing

1. The player must be behind the line of the ball.
2. He must point himself in the direction he wants the ball to go.
3. For an accurate low volley the ball should be hit on the middle but if an opponent has to be cleared then the ball is hit on the bottom to gain the necessary height.

Practice

Volley passing can be completed not only over long distances but also over short distances. It is important that players learn the rudiments of being composed when attempting a volley and this can be most usefully done over a short distance.

The ball can be served to the player at approximately 6 yards away and he must volley the ball back accurately into the hands of the server. The practice can be adapted to pretend that the server is an opponent and using the goal area the ball can be served to the player standing on the edge of the 6 yard box who must volley over the head of the server into the empty goal. For this to take place successfully, accuracy and not power is the key factor. Thus, the rudiments of success in volleying can be learned here before longer work is attempted.

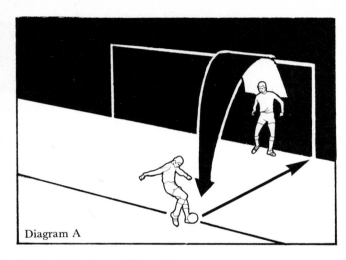

Diagram A

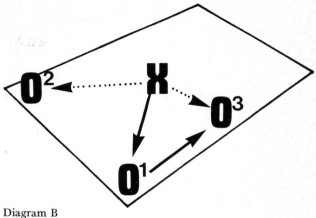

Diagram B

HOW = Techniques (Diag. A)

Under 12's
From the edge of the 6 yard box hit the post three times out of every five attempts.

Under 14's
Hit the post four times out of every five attempts.

Over 14's
Hit the post with each contact five out of five.

WHEN AND WHERE = Skill (Diag. B)

Mark out a small area roughly 10 yards square. Parent is X who serves the ball to 01 who then volleys it accurately to either 02 or 03 before X can intercept. The parent may move to cover 02 or 03 as soon as he has served the ball.

Under 14's four times out of five. Over 14's five out of five on this practice.

Volleying from defence

1. Check that the player gets behind the line of direction of the ball.
2. Check that the bottom of the ball is the part where contact is aimed for.
3. Check that the non-kicking side of the body is held firm. A common fault is that the player becomes excited and lets his non-kicking shoulder open out too far and thus he slices across the path of the ball.
4. On contact the player leans backwards and hits the

Diagram A

base of the ball back down the path upon which it has come.

Practice

Initially a good practice is to lob the ball to the young player and let it bounce once before he attempts to volley it back to or over the server. It must be said that a small garden is not the best place to practise this technique!

On a football pitch the server can stand on the corner of the penalty area and lob the ball in to the player standing on the penalty area. A good volley will go over the touch line without a bounce.

HOW = Techniques (Diag. A)

Under 12's
Volley the ball directly into touch without a bounce at least twice out of every five attempts.

Under 14's
As above, reach the touch line at least three times out of every five attempts.

Over 14's
As above, reach the touch line at least four times out of every five attempts.

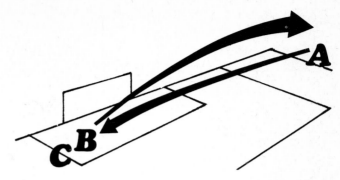

Diagram B

WHEN AND WHERE = Skill (Diag. B)

This practice is designed to test accuracy as well as length. The parent stands on the touch line and lobs the ball into the penalty area where the young player is standing near the penalty spot. An opponent C challenges him from behind.

Under 12's may let the ball bounce once before clearing high to make contact with the server without a bounce. Under 14's will aim to be successful at least three out of every five attempts in this practice. Under 14's may let the ball bounce once and should then be successful four times out of every five attempts. Alternatively they may elect to volley the ball without a bounce in which case three out of every five successful efforts is the target. Over 14's should endeavour to reach four out of five without letting the ball bounce at all. In the diagram A is the server and B is the performer.

Controlling the ball on the ground

1. Check the player has moved behind the line of the ball.
2. Ensure that as the ball comes towards the player he moves his controlling foot towards it to give braking distance.
3. As the ball reaches the player he moves the controlling foot away in the direction in which the ball is travelling to take the pace away from it.

Practice

Again use a wall or rebound surface such as a garage door.

The player stands some 10 yards away and plays the ball firmly against the rebound surface. As the ball returns he meets the rebound and controls the ball and shows that he has in fact controlled the ball by turning to face away from the ball with the ball at his feet. It is of course important to remember that players should be capable of controlling the ball with both feet and therefore practice should be undertaken first with one foot and then with the other.

HOW = Techniques (Diag. A)

Under 12's
Play the ball against the wall and control the ball with the

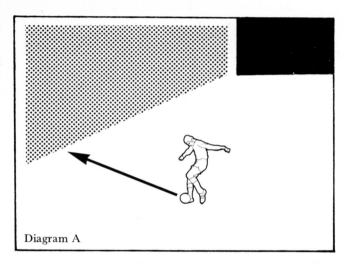

Diagram A

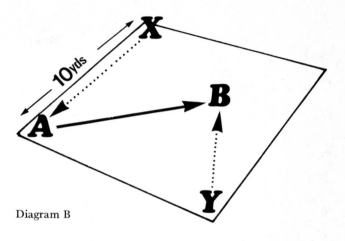

Diagram B

inside of the foot or the outside of the foot as it rebounds. Under 12's should get four out of five successes with the inside of the foot and three out of five with the outside.

Under 14's
Should score five out of five with the inside and four out of five with the outside of the foot.

Over 14's
Should score five out of five with both the inside and the outside of the foot.

WHEN AND WHERE = Skill (Diag. B)

In a small area roughly 10 yards square A and B are on the same side. X and Y are opponents who start off in the corners as indicated. A plays an accurate pass to B who must control the ball and pass it back to A immediately. X tries to cut off the pass by marking A whilst Y tries to distract B by challenging him. Every successful return counts 1 point.

Under 12's should strive to score 3 out of five successes. Under 14's four out of five. Over 14's five out of five in this practice.

Controlling with the chest

1. The player must get behind the line of the ball
2. The chest must be moved first of all towards the ball as it travels through the air towards him.
3. As the ball arrives the chest is moved in the direction in which the ball is travelling. That is to say that the chest is withdrawn and consequently hollowed. A good tip is to ask the players to breath out as the ball arrives, this hollows the chest automatically and moves it down thus making the ball come into a target area which deflects it down towards the ground for easier control.

Practice

Again here is a technique which can usefully be practised by having a partner serve the ball at the area under discussion, namely the chest.

The ball is served to the player who controls it with the chest and plays it back along the ground with a pass to the server. On a football field this practice can be completed in the goalmouth and interest can be gained by throwing the ball to the player who controls it and then attempts to score immediately by shooting. Poor control will make the ball bounce away from the player and the chance to score may be lost.

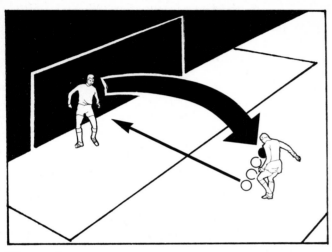

Diagram A

HOW = Techniques (Diag. A)

Under 12's
Under 12's should score 3 successes out of five.

Under 14's
Should strive for 4 out of five.

Over 14's
Should attempt to gain five out of five successes.

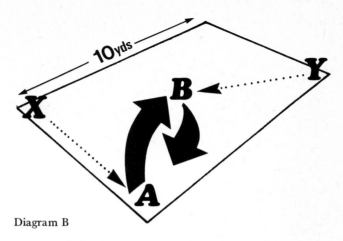

Diagram B

WHEN AND WHERE = Skill (Diag. B)

In another small area approximately 10 yards square A stands in one corner and throws the ball through the air to B. B controls with his chest andd plays the ball back to A who is challenged by X. B in turn is challenged by Y who can move as soon as the ball is thrown to him. Scoring is as follows:

Under 12's be successful 3 times out of 5. Under 14's four times out of 5. Over 14's 5 times out of 5.

When success is gained like this the position of Y can then be changed to mark immediately behind B. This puts greater pressure on B and increases the quality of the skill.

Control with the top of the foot

1. The player must be behind the line of flight of the ball.
2. The top of the foot, the controlling surface, is moved towards the ball. If the ball is dropping vertically this will mean that the foot is raised almost vertically. If the ball is travelling towards the player through the air then the foot is extended outwards and upwards to meet the line of flight.
3. As the ball arrives so the controlling foot is lowered to provide the braking distance to effect control.

Diagram A

Practice

The parent can lob the ball with his hands to the player who can then attempt to catch it using the top of the foot, lower it to the floor and effect a pass back to the server. Repeat the practice.

On a football field this can be attempted by the server standing in the 'D' at the edge of the penalty area and serving to the player who stands on the penalty spot. A good accurate pass must be made after the control is effected to reach the server inside the penalty area 'D'.

HOW = Techniques (Diag. A)

Under 12's
Catch the ball on the top of the foot and then complete the control by putting the sole of the foot on top of the ball 4 times out of 5 attempts.

Under 14's
As above. Extend the distance over which the ball is thrown and achieve at least 4 out of 5 attempts.

Over 14's
Again extend the distance further and aim to achieve 5 out of 5 successes.

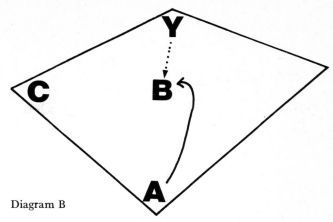

Diagram B

WHEN AND WHERE = Skill (Diag. B)

In the small area again approximately 10 yards square A lobs the ball to B. A will obviously be the parent, B the child. B catches the ball on the top of his foot and then plays it either back to A or to a colleague C. Y is an opponent who can move as soon as the ball is lobbed towards B and challenge.

Under 12's should endeavour to control the ball and make at least 3 subsequent passes.
Under 14's should endeavour to develop the passing load after a successful control to at least 10.
Over 14's should endeavour after control to pass for the maximum number of contacts that they can achieve before the ball goes out of the square or Y is successful in gaining possession.

Controlling with the head

1. The player must be in line with the ball as it travels through the air towards him.
2. The head is to be used as the controlling surface and therefore the player moves his head slightly forward to meet the ball as it comes at him.
3. As the ball arrives the head is moved again in the direction in which the ball is travelling. If the head has been moved forward as in (2) above then it can be withdrawn providing a greater braking distance to take the pace off the ball and allow it to drop down to the feet.

Practice

Again the practice that has been used for other aspects of control can be used.

That is to say the parent stands a few yards (10 or so) away from the player and lobs the ball gently towards him. The player effects the control and makes a pass back to the server to show good control.

On a football field the practice can be performed by the server standing on the penalty spot and throwing the ball to the player who stands at the edge of the D. The player controls the ball with his head and attempts to shoot past the server into the goal before the ball goes outside the D. If the ball goes outside the D then the control was poor and in a game the chance to score might well have been lost.

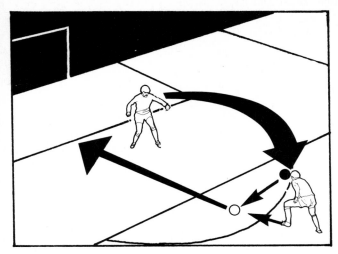

Diagram A

HOW = Techniques (Diag. A)

Under 12's
Obtain at least 3 out of 5 genuine successes.

Under 14's
At least 4 out of 5.

Over 14's
5 out of 5 successes.

WHEN AND WHERE = Skill (Diag. B)

The test is exactly the same as for Control with the Top of the Foot. Obviously the difference this time is that the ball is served to the young player's head and he must take the pace off it with his head before making the passes.

Test targets also are the same as for Control with the Top of the Foot.

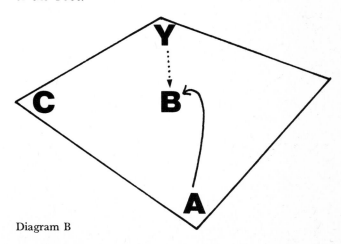

Diagram B

Controlling and turning

1. The player must be in line with the ball as it comes towards him.
2. Using the outside of the foot as the controlling surface is the best method. The outside of the foot is moved towards the ball as it travels through the air.
3. As the ball arrives the outside of the foot makes contact and withdraws slightly to take the pace off the ball. The player then turns to follow the ball as it spins off the deflecting surface past him.

Practice

On any area of grass the server throws the ball to the player who effects the control and turns to show the ball in his possession with his back ultimately presented to the server.

On a football pitch this practice can be made effective using the penalty area. The player stands on the edge of the penalty area facing his partner who stands at the edge of the 'D'. The ball is lobbed towards him and he controls and turns towards the goal shooting to score as he does so. Good control will enable the player to get in his shot well before the ball passes the penalty spot.

HOW =Techniques (Diag. A)

Under 12's
Score 3 out of 5 attempts.

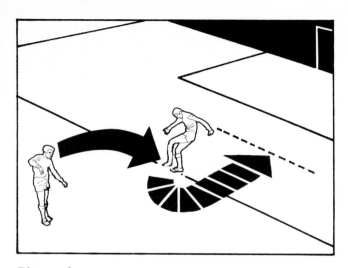

Diagram A

Under 14's
Score 4 out of 5 attempts.

Over 14's
Score 5 out of 5 attempts.

No points are scored for any age group if the shot is not made before the ball goes past the penalty spot.

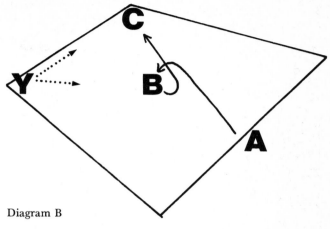

Diagram B

WHEN AND WHERE = Skill (Diag. B)

Again using a small area approximately 10 yards square. The parent A stands in the centre of the square and lobs the ball towards the child B standing approximately in the centre. An opponent Y stands in one opposite corner and a supporting player C stands in the other. B has to control the ball and pass it as he turns to C before Y can either challenge him or intercept the pass.

Under 12's should succeed 3 times out of 5. Under 14's 4 times out of 5. Over 14's 5 times out of 5.

Inside of the foot trapping

1. The player must be behind the line of the ball as it comes through the air towards him.
2. The inside of the foot is moved towards the ball as it comes through the air. Consequently the inside of the foot must be turned outwards to meet the ball.
3. On impact the inside of the foot forms a wedge with the ground into which the ball arrives. At the moment of contact the foot is moved slightly backwards to take the impetus out of the ball and ensure that it does not bounce away out of the control of the player.

Practice

A simple practice can again be produced for control by having the ball lobbed towards the player from a distance of 10 yards or so.

He must control the ball and play it back quickly to the server. On a football pitch the penalty area can be used to advantage. The server stands on the penalty spot and serves the ball to the player standing in D at the edge of the area. The control must be effected and the pass made before the ball goes outside the arc.

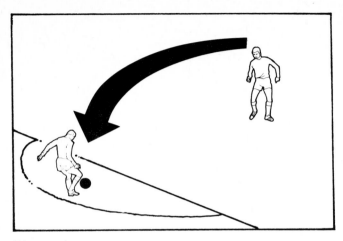

Diagram A

HOW = Techniques (Diag. A)

Under 12's
Score at least 3 out of 5 successes.

Under 14's
At least 4 out of 5 successes.

Over 14's
5 out of 5 successes should be attained at this age.

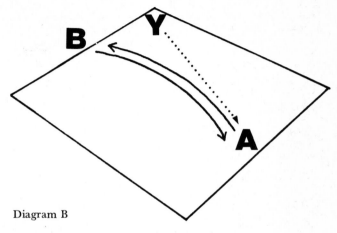

Diagram B

WHEN AND WHERE = Skill (Diag. B)

In an area approximately 10 yards square A, the parent, lobs the ball towards B who stands on the opposite side of the square. An opponent Y stands in one corner and moves to challenge B as the ball is thrown towards him. B must track the ball with the inside of his foot and play it back to A to be successful.

Under 12's should be successful at least 3 times out of 5. Under 14's 4 times out of 5. Over 14's must be successful on 5 out of 5 occasions.

Sole of the foot trapping

1. The player must get behind the line of the flight of the ball as it comes towards him.
2. As the ball comes through the air he moves himself towards the point at which the ball is to land and extends the sole of the controlling foot towards the ball.
3. As the ball arrives it enters an open sided triangle formed between the ground and the sole of the foot. Thus it is wedged into position. If the sole of the foot is relaxed slightly as the ball arrives it will be found that a more effective control is achieved.

Diagram A

Practice

Serve the ball to the player from a distance of approximately 10 yards for him to control and pass back accurately.

Earlier practices using the penalty area for alternative aspects for control can also be used and an alternative way in which a football pitch can be used is to serve the ball from the touchline towards the player who stands on the side of the penalty area. He controls the ball and plays it back quickly and accurately to the server. As the player becomes more proficient so the distance between him and the server can be extended. Eventually it is possible for the server to volley the ball out of his hands to the player receiving the ball on the opposite side of the penalty area.

However it should be stressed that this will take time and of course plenty of practice.

HOW = Techniques (Diag. A)

Under 12's
Score 3 out of 5 successes.

Under 14's
Score 4 out of 5 successes.

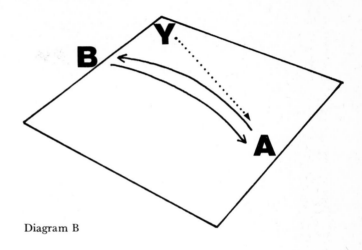

Diagram B

Over 14's
Score 5 out of 5 successes.

WHEN AND WHERE = Skill (Diag. B)

The test is the same as for inside of the foot trapping.

Again the same targets should be attained by under 12's under 14's and over 14's as are set for inside of the foot trapping.

Thigh trapping

1. The player must get behind the line of the ball as it comes towards him.
2. As the ball travels through the air the thigh is moved upwards towards it.
3. As the ball arrives the thigh is moved downwards or in the case of a flat trajectory ball moving quickly, the thigh is withdrawn in the direction in which the ball is travelling.

Practice

Here a parent can serve the ball or alternatively the player can practice on his own using a rebound surface such as a wall.

Using a wall the player throws the ball at the wall and attempts to catch the rebound on his thigh. Using the principles of control as outlined above he may in fact be able to maintain the ball on his thigh for a period of time before allowing it to descend and complete the control by putting his foot on top of it to show complete mastery of the ball.

HOW = Techniques (Diag. A)

Under 12's
Should aim to score at least 3 times out of every 5 attempts.

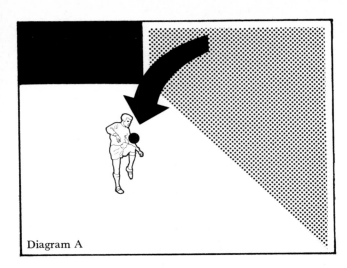

Diagram A

Under 14's
Should score 4 out of 5 attempts.

Over 14's
Should attempt to get 5 out of 5.

It is important to remember that the figures above relate to both legs. Players who can control with only 1 foot or leg are not as effective as those who can master the ball with both.

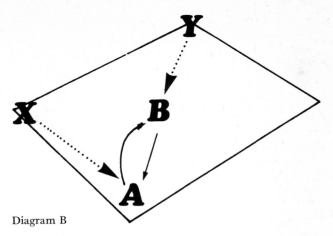

Diagram B

WHEN AND WHERE = Skill (Diag. B)

A lobs the ball through the air to B who controls with the thigh before passing back to A. X and Y are opponents. Y attempts to come in and put pressure on B whilst X makes tracks to try to intercept the pass if the control is slow or inefficient. Scoring is as follows:

Under 12's score 3 out of 5 successes. Under 14's 4 out of 5 successes. Over 14's 5 out of 5 successes.

Again the position of Y in relation to B can be changed to put more pressure on him as success is developed. Eventually Y can end up immediately behind B in a tight marking position.

Tackling from the front

1. Ensure that the ball is approached under control in terms of speed and angle. The player must endeavour to be sideways on if possible and to be approaching from an angle which forces the opponent to the side which he does not particularly wish to go towards.

2. The tackle must be made at the correct time. That is to say when the player with the ball has the ball least under his control. Young players tend to dash into

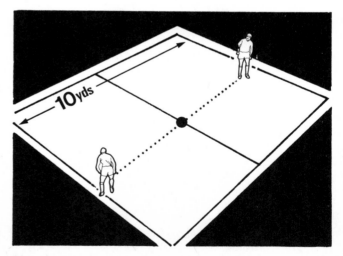

10yds

Diagram A

the tackle without thinking of the correct time when so to do.

3. In terms of winning the ball the foot must be brought into contact with the bottom of the ball and the body weight leans in and over the ball to lift it over the foot of the opponent.

Practice

The technique of tackling can be learnt by placing a ball midway between the parent and the boy.

At a given signal both attack the ball and arriving at the same time attempt to take it past the other by using a successful tackle. The parent will use discretion in the weight he puts into the tackle.

HOW = Techniques (Diag. A)

Under 12's
Should win the ball 3 out of 5 times in the tackle.

Under 14's
Should win the ball 4 out of 5 times.

Over 14's
Should win the ball 5 out of 5 times.

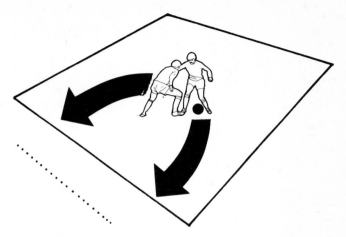

WHEN AND WHERE = Skill (Diag. B)

In a small area approximately 10 yards x 10 yards a game of 1 v 1 is developed. In this way the object is to dribble the ball to end at the opposite side of the square without the opponent being able to prevent you so doing. To show good control the player must stand with his foot on the opponents line when he has defeated his opponent in the tackle. Here obviously the test is to defeat the opponent and it matters not whether the players are under 12, under 14 or over 14. The rudiments of a real game are present here and the winner is the one with the most points at the end of the specified number of attempts or time period.

Tackling from the side

1. Judge the time to tackle when you are near enough to the opponent and the ball is not exactly under his control. If incorrect timing is used as the tackle is made the opponent will be fouled as contact will be made with him. At worst he will be able to pursue the ball with the defender on the floor and out of the game.
2. The foot furthest from the opponent is used to win the ball.
3. If possible the nearest foot is used as a pivot to swing round and pull the defender into a front tackling position.
4. However if (3) above is not possible then the foot furthest away from the ball is used to push the ball away from the opponent and this is especially effective if the opponent is running with the ball near the touch line. The object is to play the ball into touch.

Practice

The parent stands with the ball with the young defender slightly behind him. He starts to jog away from the young player who pursues him and initially practises to get the foot furthest away from the ball into contact with the ball to push it away to the side of his parent.

As he becomes more proficient in this then the practice is extended to encourage him to get into a tackle whereby he

Diagram A

can pivot on the nearest foot and win the ball whilst retaining his balance and take it away in the opposite direction past his parent.

HOW = Techniques (Diag. A)

Under 12's
Win the ball and play it into touch or over the agreed line 3 times out of 5.

Under 14's
As above. Win the ball 4 times out of 5.

Over 14's
As above. Win the ball 5 times out of 5.

WHEN AND WHERE = Skill (Diag. B)

B is the parent who moves with the ball towards a line 10 yards or so away from him. A is the child who attempts to dispossess him from a starting position behind the ball. Thus he must either tackle from the side or swiftly get into a front tackling position.

Under 12's should win the ball at least 3 times out of 5 before the parent reaches the end line. Under 14's 4 times out of 5. Over 14's 5 times out of 5.

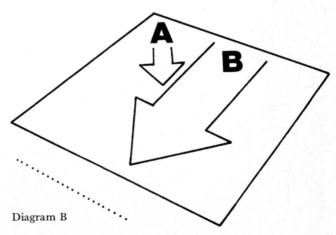

Diagram B

Running with the ball

1. Players should be encouraged to run with the ball only when there is no advantage to be gained by making a pass or taking the opportunity to shoot.
2. When running with the ball players should be encouraged initially to keep the ball close to them by pushing the ball only so far in front of them as they need to do to be able to look up and assess the situation.
3. Players should be encouraged to run with the ball using

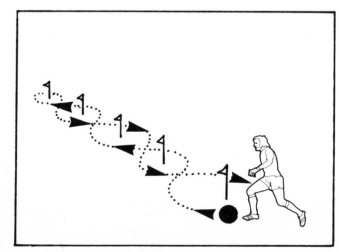

Diagram A

the inside, outside and top of the foot as the points with which to make contact. Again the important thing to stress is that when running with the ball the head is not always looking at it. The head looks at the ball as contact is made, as the ball goes away the head comes up to look around to see if the possibility of a pass exists.

Practice

An old but nevertheless sound practice to teach the basic rudiments of running with the ball is to mark out with cricket stumps or some such implements a course of 5 obstacles over 50 yards.

The player then runs in and out of the obstacles with the ball before returning to the starting line. The parent should insist as the player is running that the head keeps coming up to look about.

HOW = Techniques (Diag. A)

Under 12's
Complete the course without missing any flag out.

Under 14's
Complete the course when timed by the parent. The object of the test is to reduce the time taken to get a record time.

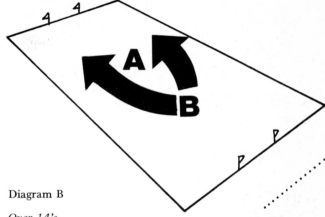

Diagram B

Over 14's
As for under 14's. Again attempting to reduce the time taken to complete the course.

WHEN AND WHERE = Skill (Diag.B)

This test is the same as for the test for tackling from the front. A and B are opposed to each other and A can of course be the parent. B attempts to take the ball past A to reach the end line and control the ball with his foot on top of it. The parent tries to do the same in the opposite direction, thus a game of 1 v 1 is developed. For all ages the target is the same, to be more successful than the opponent.

Screening the ball

1. The ball must be kept under control and as far away from the opponent as possible.
2. The body must be turned sideways and if possible the ball played with the outside of the foot furthest away from the opponent.
3. The ball must be kept within playing distance of the player screening the ball or the laws of the game are broken.

Practice

The parent lobs the ball through the air to the young player who traps it with the outside of his foot.

This turns him into a sideways on position. From this position he now runs towards the parent in a sideways on position playing the ball with the outside of his foot as he covers the ground. On arrival he leaves the ball with the parent and returns to his position for the ball to be re-thrown to him. This is a good practice for teaching the basic techniques of screening since not only is the sideways on position attained and the player encouraged to play the ball with the outside of his foot from this position but also covering ground it is easy to see whether he is keeping the ball in playing distance at all times.

This is the hardest aspect of screening to develop especially when players are moving. Players should be encouraged to move when screening the ball as this confuses the picture

Diagram A

further for the opponent who may be encouraged to make an ill-timed tackle and then be beaten on the turn or alternatively give away a free kick through making contact with the player and not the ball.

HOW = Techniques (Diag. A)

Under 12's
Cover the distance with the ball fully under control at least 3 times out of every 5 attempts successfully.

Under 14's
As above. Cover the distance at least 4 times out of every 5 attempts successfully.

Over 14's
Cover the distance 5 times out of 5 successfully.

WHEN AND WHERE = Skill (Diag. B)

In a small area approximately 10 yards by 10 yards the parent, B, stands behind the player, A, who has the ball. A has to cover the diagonal across the area to arrive with the ball under control in the opposite corner.

Under 14's should reach 4 out of 5 successes. Over 14's five out of 5 successes.

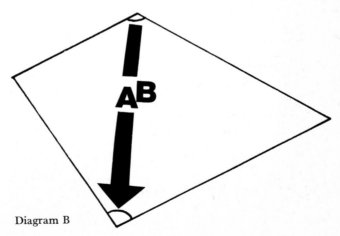

Diagram B

Heading for goal

1. Get behind the line of the ball as it comes through the air.
2. Aim to meet the ball above its mid-line with the forehead.
3. Time the jump to be at the highest point as the ball arrives and bring the head, neck and body through and down onto the top half of the ball.

Diagram A

Practice

Again it is useful to either improvise a goal or go on to a football pitch.

The player stands on the edge of the penalty area and the parent stands on the goal line at the edge of the 6 yard box. The young player begins to run diagonally towards the goal as shown in diagram A. The parent lobs the ball for him to head into goal. The ball should be headed down into goal and if possible should bounce on or around the goal line as it enters the net.

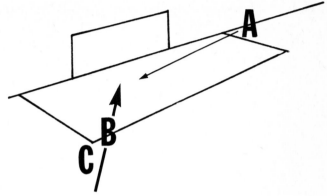

Diagram B

WHEN AND WHERE = Skill (Diag. B)

The parent A serves the ball as in the earlier practice for the player B to attack and score. The difference is this time that an opponent C is introduced who starts slightly behind B but puts him under pressure as he goes in to try and score. A goalkeeper can make the practice even more difficult and turn it into a real match situation.

In such a situation, under 12's should score 2 times out of 5 attempts. Under 14's 3 out of 5 attempts. Over 14's 4 out of 5 attempts.

HOW = Techniques (Diag. A)

Under 12's
Be successful on 3 out of 5 headed attempts.

Under 14's
Be successful on 4 out of 5 attempts.

Over 14's
Be successful 5 out of 5 attempts.

Heading from defence

1. Get behind the line of the ball.
2. Attack the ball and take off on one foot for maximum height.
3. Aim for the bottom of the ball and head up for height and distance. The points regarding heading, as mentioned in Heading For Goal, should also be taken into consideration. In Heading From Defence height and distance are the main considerations. Heading the ball down to the edge of the penalty area simply will not do.

Practice

The parent lobs the ball in to the young player who attacks the bottom of the ball to gain height and distance.

The object initially is to head the ball over and beyond the parent. The parent can make the practice competitive by leaping to make himself bigger to force a higher, longer header from the player. The biggest problem in heading is establishing confidence, so it is often a good idea to allow players to attack the ball held on the palm of the hand of a parent in the early stages. Thus they become confident that the ball will not hurt them and attack the base of the ball. Constant practice will then help them to develop the one foot take off to gain maximum height and distance.

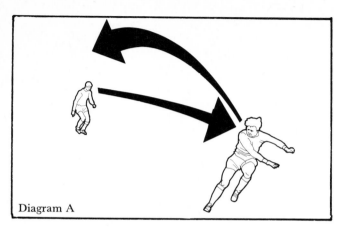

Diagram A

HOW = Techniques (Diag. A)

Under 12's
The parent serves the ball from 6 yards away and the boy attempts to head the ball over him at least twice out of every 5 attempts.

Under 14's
As above. The distance is extended to 9 yards and at least 4 out of every 5 attempts are required for success.

Over 14's
As above. The distance is extended to 12 yards and 5 out of 5 headers should pass over the head of the serving parent.

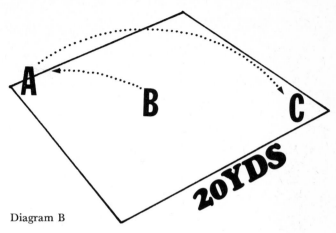

Diagram B

WHEN AND WHERE = Skill (Diag. B)

Mark out an approximately 20 yards square. The parent B stands in the centre of this area and lobs the ball towards the player A who stands in one corner. The parent then becomes an opponent, moving in to challenge A who has to head over him to his partner C standing in the opposite corner. C controls the ball as it arrives by trapping it. Thus a linked practice between heading and trapping is developed. A has to clear B and get the ball to C without a bounce for a success.

Under 12's aim for 2 successes at least from 5 attempts. Under 14's at least 4 times out of 5 attempts. Over 14's 5 out of 5.

Inswinging corners

1. Approach the ball in a balanced position as for a long high pass. The ball should be placed in the corner of the quadrant nearest to the goalpost. That is to say at the point where the quadrant cuts the goal-line.
2. The non-kicking side shoulder should point at the goalpost and the ball is struck below the mid-line and slightly to the infield side of centre in order that inspin is imparted to the ball thus bringing it in towards the goal.

Diagram A

3. The point of contact of the foot is of course the instep striking straight through the ball.

Practice

Practice for corners is most significantly done on a football field or alternatively on an area of ground where two posts are put in.

The posts can be simple canes 8 yards apart but the critical factor is the distance from the nearest cane to the player. Young players will of course be able to strike the ball over less distance than older players and so the distance can be extended as they grow older, or become successful in reaching the cane or goalposts.

HOW = Techniques (Diag. A)

Under 12's
Score 1 point by getting the ball into the 18 yard box without a bounce and 3 points for reaching the 6 yard box without a bounce.

Under 14's
Score the same.

Over 14's
Score 3 points only when the ball lands in the 6 yard box but no points if it does not make this distance.

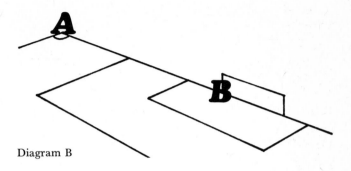

Diagram B

Targets are as follows
Under 12's score 7 points or more from five attempts.
Under 14's score 11 points or more from five attempts.
Over 14's score 12 points or more from five attempts.

WHEN AND WHERE = Skill (Diag. B)

A takes the corner and the parent stands just inside the near post at B. The target is for the parent to either head the ball into the goal or to catch the ball before it bounces, at this point.

Under 12's should reach at least once out of every five attempts. Under 14's at least three times out of every five attempts. Over 14's should reach five times out of every five attempts.

Long throws

1. The hands must be behind the ball and spread out.
2. The player must co-ordinate his feet, back and hands together to produce the right technical trajectory to satisfy the laws of the game and gain distance.
3. The feet are placed on or behind the line to give a good base of support and the back and legs move backwards to swing forwards with impetus to gain the required distance. With young players the important thing is first of all to gain the correct technical execution and then build for distance from that point.

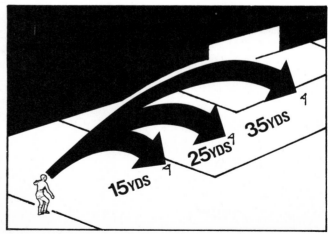

Diagram A

Practice

Using a good distance of garden, or better still a football pitch, technique practice can be developed to produce confidence, fluidity and distance.

The player stands on the touch-line (in a garden mark a line). His feet must be on or behind the line. The parent marks out the distances as shown and acts as 'judge'. In addition care should be taken to see that the key points listed opposite are followed.

It is often amazing to see the number of young (and older) players who cannot throw a ball in correctly. Here there can be no excuse other than lack of practice. Encouraging distance *can* encourage good technique. It avoids the 'jerky' movement which is against the laws and also encourages the player to take the ball well back — a common fault in young players is to make throw ins from a point where the ball starts immediately above the top of the head, or even worse — the forehead!

HOW = Techniques (Diag. A)

Under 12's
With five attempts score 1 point every time the 15 yard target is passed. Score two points everytime the 25 yard target is passed. The target score for Under 12's to reach out of every five attempts is 6 points.

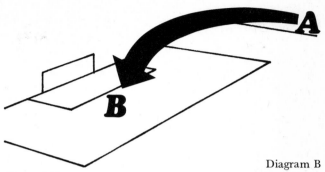

Diagram B

Under 14's
With the same scoring tally have a target of 8 points or more.

Over 14's
A target of 10 points from every five attempts is set for the same practice.

WHEN AND WHERE = Skill (Diag. B)

Player stands at A and throws the ball in to parent standing at B. If the ball reaches the parent without a bounce then 3 points are scored. If the ball bounces once two points are scored, and if the ball bounces twice 1 point is scored. If the ball bounces more than twice no points are scored.

Targets for the five attempts are exactly as in the practice for techniques.

Low drive

1. A balanced approach is essential, with eye on the ball.
2. On contact the player should aim to hit squarely through the ball and along the middle line in order to keep it down to pass underneath the cross bar. To get the ball between the posts the player should ensure that the non-kicking side is lined up with the goal and held there on contact. If the non-kicking shoulder opens out too wide, then the ball may be sliced or dragged past one of the posts.
3. For power, which is the second requirement to accuracy in shooting, follow through is required. A good contact on the ball with the foot following through in the direction that the ball is going provides the power because the backswing prior to the follow through will have consequently been faster and thus the speed of the ball will be quicker.

Practice

The player stands facing the goal and the ball is rolled towards him. He comes in and strikes the ball aiming to score.

On a football pitch the parent may stand on the goal line and play the ball towards the player who stands on the edge of the penalty area. As the ball is rolled the player advances towards the ball and shoots with one touch only allowed. Shooting opportunities come to both feet, so practice

Diagram A

should be from both sides of the goal. Players should be encouraged to use both feet.

HOW = Techniques (Diag. A)

Under 12's
Score with at least 3 out of every 5 shots.

Under 14's
Score with at least 4 out of every 5 shots.

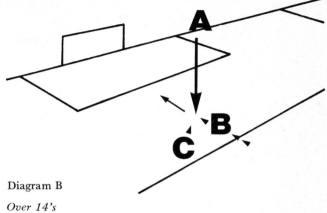

Diagram B

Over 14's
Score on every occasion.

WHEN AND WHERE = Skill (Diag. B)

The practice is the same as for techniques with exception that an opponent C is introduced. C stands at the edge of the penalty area D and as the ball is played towards B comes in to challenge. B must ignore his challenge and score as before. Again an additional player can be used as a goalkeeper to make the practice even more realistic.

Under 12's should score 3 out of 5. Under 14's should score 4 out of 5. Over 14's 5 out of 5.

Bending the ball

1. The object in bending the ball is to get it round an obstacle.
2. On contact the ball is either struck to the right or the left of the middle vertical line. A ball struck with the inside of the right foot on the outside of the ball will have anti-clockwise spin imparted to it. A ball struck with the inside of the left foot on the outside of the ball will have clockwise spin imparted to it. Thus a right foot shot so struck will swerve to the kicker's left whilst a left foot shot so struck will swerve to the kicker's right.

Diagram A

3. A ball struck with the outside of the right foot on the inside of the ball will have clockwise spin imparted to it and a ball struck with the outside of the left foot on the inside will have an anti-clockwise spin on it. Thus such a shot with the right foot will swerve to the kicker's right and such a shot with the left foot will swerve to the kicker's left.

Practice

The player stands facing a goal and has an obstacle placed between himself and the goal in a direct line.

The object of the practice is for the player to swerve the ball around the obstacle or parent to get it into the goal. A ball which is not struck with swerve will hit the obstacle and not count as a goal. Again it is important to stress that practice is taken with both feet. Practice should include playing the ball with both the inside and the outside of the foot as outlined above to practise both types of swerve with both feet.

HOW = Techniques (Diag. A)

Under 12's
Swerve the ball around the obstacle at least twice out of every 5 attempts.

Under 14's
At least 3 times out of every 5 attempts.

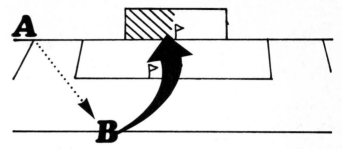

Diagram B

Over 14's
4 out of every 5 attempts.

WHEN AND WHERE = Skill (Diag. B)

The parent A stands on the goal line roughly at a point where the penalty area joins it. He serves the ball towards B and a skittle, or similar obstacle, is placed in the path of the player B and another skittle or obstacle is placed on the goal line. The player has to play the ball round the obstacle and into the shaded area on Diagram B.

Under 12's should score at least 2 out of 5 successes. Under 14's at least 3 out of 5 successes. Over 14's 4 out of 5 successes on this test. This is not an easy test but perseverance is often well rewarded.

Half-volley shooting

1. The player's striking foot must be in line with the ball as it comes towards him.
2. In order for the ball to go into the goal it is important that the player keeps over the top of the ball.
3. Contact is made as the ball just touches the ground. Contact is made with the instep and the instep makes contact on the ball at a point on the mid-line. The body of the kicker is over the ball as much as possible in order to facilitate contact being made on the mid-line and consequently the ball is kept down.
4. Normal other points of volleying obtain and the non-kicking side shoulder must point squarely in the direction that the ball is required to travel. If the player opens his shoulder too much then he will pull the ball across the face of the goal or alternatively slice it without making a good square contact.

Practice

The ball is lobbed towards the player who comes in to meet it as it touches the floor and plays it into goal.

On a football pitch the parent or server can stand on the goal line and lob the ball towards the player who stands on the penalty spot. He moves into the path of the ball and plays it on the half volley into the goal.

Diagram A

HOW = Techniques (Diag. A)

Under 12's
Should score 3 out of 5.

Under 14's
Should score 4 out of 5.

Over 14's
Should score 5 out of 5.

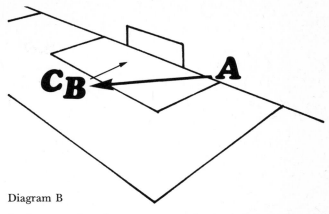

Diagram B

Again remember these targets are for both feet. In football the ball comes through the air at both sides of the goal and both feet should be developed as full as possible.

WHEN AND WHERE = Skill (Diag. B)

The practice situation is the same as in Diag. A but an opponent C is introduced. A, the parent, lobs the ball to B as C challenges from a position just behind him. B has little time in which to control the ball and therefore attempts to meet it on the half volley and shoot into goal.

Under 12's should score 3 out of 5. Under 14's 4 out of 5. Over 14's 5 out of 5.

Volleying to score

1. The player must get his striking foot behind the line of the ball as it comes through the air towards him.
2. The non-kicking side shoulder is fixed at the point on the goal where the ball is required to be sent.
3. In order to keep the ball beneath the cross bar it is important to make contact on the mid-line of the ball. Consequently the player leans into the ball and raises his hip to ensure that a square contact is made up the ball.

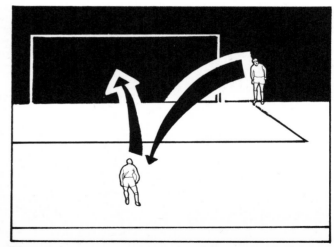

Diagram A

Practice

The ball is lobbed through the air to the player who meets it before it bounces and strikes it into goal.

On a football pitch the practice can be performed by the parent lobbing the ball towards the player from the point where the 6 yard box cuts the goal line. As he lobs the ball he then moves into goal to act as goalkeeper. The player comes to meet the ball and volleys it at the goal attempting to direct it towards the far side of the goal away from his parent who is moving to take up the position of acting goalkeeper. Shots which miss the goal by going wide mean that the player has probably opened his non-kicking shoulder too wide or closed it too much. Shots which go over the bar mean that the player has hit under the mid-line of the ball. Thus the parent can diagnose exactly what the fault was on each occasion.

HOW = Techniques (Diag. A)

Under 12's
Should endeavour to score 3 times out of 5.

Under 14's
4 times out of 5.

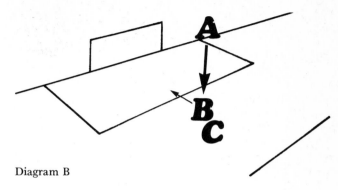

Diagram B

Over 14's
5 times out of 5.

Under 14's and over 14's may like to endeavour to score from a point at the edge of the penalty area and the greater distance of course increases the difficulty of the task.

WHEN AND WHERE = Skill (Diag. B)

An exactly similar situation to half volley skill practice is developed. Diag. B illustrates this.

Targets are again under 12's to score at least 3 times out of every 5 attempts. Under 14's 4 times out of every 5 attempts. Over 14's 5 out of 5 attempts.

Volleying with back to goal

1. The foot selected must be thrown at the back of the ball from the performer's point of view.
2. The ankle is relaxed to flatten the foot and keep the ball beneath the foot and have an effect of pulling downwards on the ball to keep it below the bar.
3. The player pulls his leg towards him on contact and over his shoulder as he leans and falls away towards the goal.

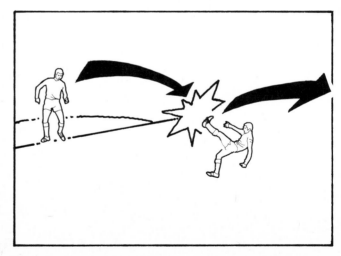

Diagram A

Practice

Volleying back to goal is an advanced but enjoyable skill for youngsters to practise.

The secret of success is the timing of the contact on the ball. If the contact is too early the ball goes straight up but if the contact is too late it goes down into the ground and will perhaps be saved. Correct timing takes the ball over the shoulder and directly into the goal. Practice can be effected on a football field by the parent standing in the 'D' of the penalty area facing the child who stands on the penalty spot. The ball is lobbed towards the child who attempts to pull it over his shoulder into the goal. True success is achieved when the ball goes immediately into the goal without a bounce. Again both feet should be practised.

HOW = Techniques (Diag. A)

Under 12's
Score twice out of every 5 attempts.

Under 14's
Score 3 times out of every 5 attempts.

Over 14's
Score 4 times out of every 5 attempts.

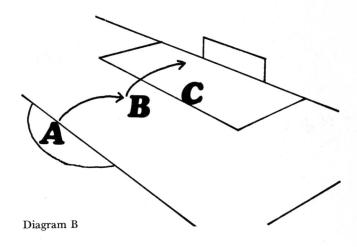

Diagram B

WHEN AND WHERE = Skill (Diag. B)

The parent A lobs the ball from a position in the D towards the player B standing on the penalty spot. An opponent C is positioned on the edge of the 6 yard box. He can elect whether to challenge the kicker as he volleys over his head or to drop back onto the goal line to make a save.

Under 12's should score 2 times out of 5 attempts. Under 14's 3 times out of 5 attempts. Over 14's 4 times out of 5 attempts.

Goalkeeping–diving to save

Diagram A

1. The important thing is to spring through the air and not flop onto the ball.
2. The player must endeavour to get two surfaces, hands and body, behind the ball whenever possible. Thus diving is a sideways action and not a cat-like drop on top of the ball.
3. As soon as contact is made on the ball the hands pull it into the body for extra protection and safety.
4. If it is not possible to pull the ball into the body then at full stretch the hands may be used as a deflecting surface to angle the ball away for a corner behind the post.

Practice

The parent faces the young player some 10 yards away in a goal or an improvised goal made of canes.

He throws the ball from this position to the side of the keeper who has to dive to save. Service is important here especially in the early stages as the ball should be served below waist height for the goalkeeper. The goalkeeper dives and attempts to catch and pull the ball into his body. However if the ball is served to such an extent that this is not possible then he must push it behind the post. In such a case if he is unsuccessful at pushing the ball behind the post but maintains it within the field of play then the parent will move forward and attempt to score by playing the ball into the goal.

Here the young goalkeeper must try to come out and smother the ball at the feet of the parent. In diving to save it is important to practise with balls served to both the right and left hand side of the goalkeeper.

HOW = Techniques (Diag. A)

Under 12's
Save at least 3 times from every 5 attempts.

Under 14's
Reach 4 out of every 5 attempts.

Over 14's
Reach 5 out of every 5 attempts.

Again it must be stressed that the ball must be served to both sides of the goalkeeper in order to give practice at diving to both left and right.

WHEN AND WHERE = Skill (Diag. B)

The parent C lobs the ball past A and B who stand back to back on the edge of the penalty area D. A and B challenge to reach the ball and shoot. Whichever player, A or B, reaches the ball gets in the shot. The goalkeeper therefore knows that a shot is coming but does not know which player is going to put in the shot or to which side of his goal it is going to go.

Consequently he is faced with many of the problems that he will have to cope with in a game. The goalkeeper should endeavour to make saves as follows:

Under 12's 2 out of 5 successes. Under 14's 3 out of 5 successes. Over 14's 4 out of 5 successes.

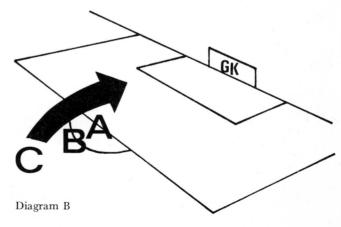

Diagram B

Goalkeeper punching to clear

1. A goalkeeper punching needs maximum power for height and distance. He gets this by exploding his arms outwards and keeping his fists or fist tightly closed. Two fists are obviously preferable to one.
2. Contact is made on the ball at the bottom in order to get the height. The hands move forward to meet the ball in order that distance may be achieved.
3. Goalkeepers will usually make two handed punches to high balls which come down the middle of the

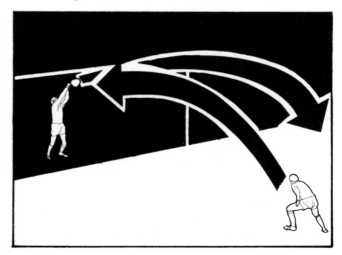

Diagram A

pitch. It is important that goalkeepers remember that only where they are under pressure is punching best, but that otherwise it is best to catch.

Practice

The ball is lobbed towards the young player who punches the ball over the head of the server.

On a football pitch the server would stand on the edge of the penalty area and lob the ball in towards the goal. He would then follow his pass in as the goalkeeper attempts to punch it over the top of him. The practice ends if the ball is punched outside the penalty area.

HOW = Techniques (Diag. A)

Under 12's
Score 2 out of 5 successes in clearing the opponent.

Under 14's
Score 3 out of 5 successes in clearing the opponent and gaining distance out of the penalty area.

Over 14's
As for under 14's, but score 5 out of 5 successes.

It is important that as boys grow older they realise that when punching to clear, height and distance are vital everytime they punch.

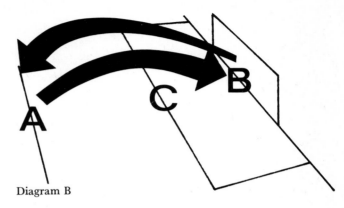

Diagram B

WHEN AND WHERE = Skill (Diag. B)

Parent A stands on the edge of the penalty area and lobs a high ball in towards goal where the player B comes to meet it, challenged by opponent C who starts from a position on the edge of the 6 yard box. The goalkeeper advances to meet the lobbed ball as C attempts to head it into goal. He is thus under pressure and if the service is accurate will have to punch clear. It should be stressed that if the service is not accurate and the ball is lobbed well over C then the goalkeeper should be encouraged to catch the ball. Targets are as follows:

Under 12's should endeavour to clear at least 2 times out of every 5 attempts successfully. Under 14's at least 3 times out of 5 successfully. Over 14's must be successful every time they elect to punch.

Goalkeeper clearing over the bar

1. The goalkeeper must get behind the line of the ball and must assess that he is close to his goal and under pressure from opponents which makes it impossible for him to catch the ball.
2. His eyes are fixed on the ball and his body turns to face the goal.
3. As the ball arrives his arms and hands push the ball firmly over the bar. He does not slap at the ball. This is a common fault in young goalkeepers.

Diagram A

Practice

The ball is lobbed towards the young goalkeeper standing in the goal who moves to meet it and push it over the bar.

Obviously this practice is best undertaken on a football field where the partner or parent stands on the edge of the penalty area and lobs the ball across the face of the goal to the young goalkeeper. The goalkeeper on his line moves towards the ball and turns to push it over the top of the bar as indicated.

HOW = Techniques (Diag. A)

Under 12's
Play the ball over the bar at least 3 times out of every 5 attempts.

Under 14's
Play the ball over the bar at least 4 times out of every 5 attempts.

Over 14's
Play the ball over the bar at least 5 times out of every 5 attempts.

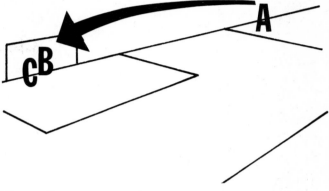

Diagram B

WHEN AND WHERE = Skill (Diag. B)

Parent A lobs the ball in towards goal for the player B to attempt to clear. Opponent C stands next to the goalkeeper marking him tightly. Thus the goalkeeper is under severe challenge and as the ball is close to goal will not be able to risk catching the ball. He must turn it over the bar.

Under 12's should be successful 3 times out of every 5 attempts. Under 14's 3 times out of every 5 attempts. Over 14's should be successful on every occasion that the ball is served into them.

Goalkeeper distributing the ball

1. Throwing the ball means a co-ordination of eyes, arms and legs. Legs give the firm base required to make the throw.
2. The non-throwing arm is outstretched to give balance.
3. The body's centre of gravity is lowered by bending the knee.
4. The throwing arm comes through as if one was throwing a javelin in the direction that the goalkeeper is facing. Alternatively the ball may be bowled out rather in the manner of a cricketer bowling at a batsman.

   In both cases the hand position is behind the ball in order to give thrust.
5. After the ball has gone the goalkeeper follows through with his throwing arm and watches the flight in order that he may assess his next movement. If his throw is successful then he will move forward to support the throw, but if it is unsuccessful then he will have to assess his next movement according to the position of the opponent who successfully intercepts.

Practice

The goalkeeper throws the ball from any position to hit his parent who moves about in order that different angles and distances may be achieved.

On a football field, placing stakes at various distances for the young player to attempt to strike with his accurate throw produces a good practice. For short accurate throws where no opponents are between the goalkeeper and his team mate the goalkeeper may bowl the ball out underarm.

HOW = Techniques (Diag. A)

The player has to distribute the ball and hit sticks or skittles placed in the ground at various distances away from him. He is encouraged to use different methods of throwing the ball for the various distances. An exact hit on a stick counts 3 points.

Under 12's
Should endeavour to score 6 points out of 5 attempts.

Under 14's
Should endeavour to score 9 points out of 5 attempts.

Over 14's
Should endeavour to score 12 points out of 5 attempts.

Where the skittle is thought to be a too small a target, then a gap of approximately 6 feet can be used as a target and a ball passing through the gap attains the points.

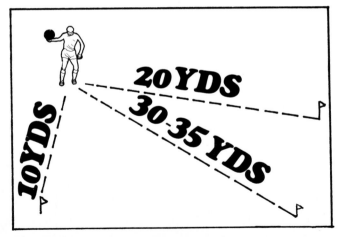

Diagram A

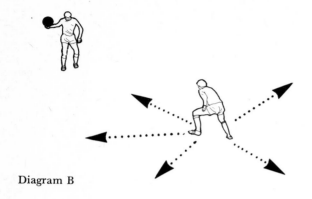

Diagram B

WHEN AND WHERE = Skill (Diag. B)

In a game the goalkeeper has to hit a target, that is to say a member of his own side. In this practice the parent becomes a member of the boy's side and moves about as the ball is thrown. The parent plays the ball back to the goalkeeper before moving off to another position. The player receives the ball and immediately distributes accurately to the feet of the parent.

Under 12's should be accurate with 3 out of 5 distributions. Under 14's 4 out of 5 distributions. Over 14's 5 out of 5 distributions. The practice should be done over varying distances sometimes the parent coming quite close and sometimes being a considerable distance, up to 35 yards, away from the player.

Teaching the
basics of team play

Teaching the basics of team play

The use of small sided games

First of all one must identify what one means by the term 'Small Sided Games'. In this respect one is really dealing with games of less than 11-A-Side. It has been established that Association Football, in its adult form, is obviously played between two teams of 11, but that this is not necessarily the best medium for teaching young players the basic skills and development of the game in its widest sense. Consider for a moment a game of Association Football played between two teams of 11-A-Side. Let us, for purpose of argument, take a full League game which lasts for 90 minutes. In practice, school boy games are, of course, often less than the 90 minute period and rightly so. However, in a 90 minute game it has been calculated that the ball is roughly out of play for 30 minutes thus providing an opportunity for involvement by all players in detailed contact with the ball of 60 minutes. Let us therefore suppose that each side has possession for roughly the same amount of time, in other words, 30 minutes each. Since each side has 11 players we can therefore divide 30 minutes by 11 as being roughly the mean average contact time that each individual will have on the ball. Thus we see that for something less than 3 minutes in every full game the player is actually involved with the ball.

Now one knows that much of Association Football is obviously to do with not being on the ball all the time. Knowing how and where to run when one's side has the ball, and also knowing how and where to run when the opponents have the ball, are of vital importance.

However it is of course of supreme importance that when the ball does come to you you have the ability to make it do what you require. All running and no technique makes for dull players!

Yet this is the problem you create if you merely play 11 v 11 football, for it is obviously inefficient to expect players to learn the basic skills and control required when they may only have the ball for less than 3 minutes out of every 90 minutes 'practice'.

Whatever else we know about skill learning, we know that constant repetition practice is a good source of technique development. Thus technique work, as has already been identified, will play an important part in the development of the young player and this will be extremely important, at very young ages, as is explained later on in the book according to the child's own development as a person as opposed merely to a player of Association Football. Also, as has been said, skill practice must involve opponents and supporting players and indeed these situations could be fairly described as uneven games of a small sided nature. For example, what else but a small sided game is 2 v 1 or 4 v 2 etc. Details of how to use these sort of practices have already been given according to the specific basic skills and techniques of the game in the earlier part of the book.

Yet there are also important lessons to be learned not

merely concerned with controlling and manipulating the ball itself.

As has already been stated, for 87 minutes out of every game a player is probably involved in moving into position either to receive the ball from supporting players or to deny the ball being progressed by opponents. Consequently therefore work must be done from the earliest age to create some sort of understanding of team play. It is here in establishing good sound principles of play that the small sided team game will be seen to its best advantage. Nevertheless small sided team games of 3 v 3 and 5 v 5 will of course also, by their very definition, afford good opportunities for the development of basic skills of the game.

Coaching In Small Sided Games—What to Look For

What are the sort of principles upon which Association Football is founded, above and beyond a knowledge of basic skill in ball manipulation?

1. Ball Possession—The Vital Factor

The first concept which must be established and understood by all who would play the game successfully and for maximum enjoyment is that ball possession determines everything. For example when our side has the ball, whatever the number on our shirt may be, we are attacking players, and likewise when the opposition attains possession, whatever the number on our shirt may be, we are defenders. It is of course easy to say this but that in itself is not sufficient. For players must understand how to defend and how to attack especially when they themselves are not in possession of the ball, in order that they may be both successful in assisting their team mates to make attacking progress and also in denying progress to the opposition.

2. Defence and Attack

One leading football authority has established the principles of the game as follows:-

(a) *Defence*
   (i) Creating pressure on opponents in possession of the ball.
   (ii) Supporting the player on your side who is establishing the pressure on the opponent with the ball.
   (iii) Covering and marking opponents who are attacking by making runs at your goal without the ball.

(b) *Attacking Play*
   (i) Supporting the player on the ball.
   (ii) Attacking without the ball by providing (1) runs at the opponents goal and (2) by establishing the full width of the attacking front.

A. Defence

Let us look therefore at some of the activities which could be selected by a parent looking after a group of, shall we say 6 boys playing a game of 3 v 3.

1. Encouraging players to effect defence by pressurizing the player on the ball.
   (a) The establishment of the distance from the man with the ball by the player attempting to pressurize is important. The player should not be so far away from the ball that the opponent can raise his head easily and play the ball past him. However, he should not commit himself, without thinking, to tackling to win the ball, but rather should station himself at a position which forces the player on the ball to have his head and eyes fixed on it. In such a way the attacking play is effectively cut down since the player's vision is restricted.
   (b) The point above referred really, to the distance of the marking player from the ball but it is still possible to obtain the correct distance and be beaten if one approaches on the wrong angle. Players should be encouraged to make their approach at an angle which prevents the opponent from playing the ball easily to supporting players.

2. Providing Cover for the Pressuring Player
   (a) Here again the correct angle and distance of support to the pressuring player are important. It is no use for the covering player to be so far away from the defender who is pressurizing the ball that the player on the ball can dribble past the first player and retain possession and be able to attack the second player. But neither is it acceptable for the player to be so close that one ball may be played past them both enabling the dribbling player to move onto it and thus put two of them out of the game.
   (b) Establishing the principle of distance and angle clearly identifies the function of the covering player. He is there to assist the pressuring player in both cutting down the amount of vision of the opponent and also giving opportunity for the ball to be won by the first player tackling. Consequently the angle of the covering player will be according to the angle of approach and pressurizing that is taken up by the first player.
   (c) Once again all players other than the first player, who is pressurizing, and the second player, who is covering, and in this case there will only be one, must be ensuring that they are achieving goal side positions to provide effective support and balance should either of the first two or both, be beaten.

3. Covering Players Making Runs Without the Ball
Here we have established already that player 1 will be concerned with pressurizing, and player 2 concerned with giving him support by covering. Player 3 therefore must take the responsibility for other opponents moving forward to attack the goal without the ball. Consequently he will be returning onto the goal side of the ball in such a way as to make the most effective line of defence. In this way therefore he will be returning directly towards the goal on the shortest line possible.

being taken down the line and 03 attacks without the ball. Thus 3 makes a run to recover position on the goal side of the ball. Suppose 01 manages to pass to 02 as below, defence strength is maintained by re-adjustment as below:-

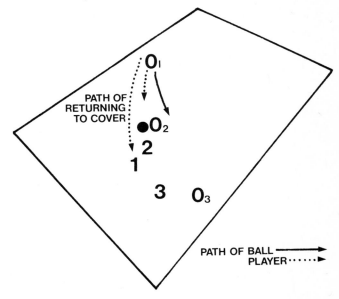

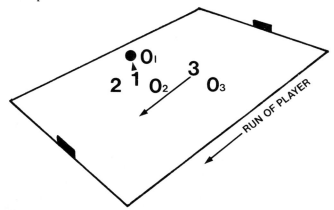

Here No 1 is forcing the player 01 towards the touch-line. No 2 has taken up a supporting position to prevent the ball

2 is now 'pressuring' the ball. 1 is covering him and 3 has recovered.

Now suppose a pass is made to 03.

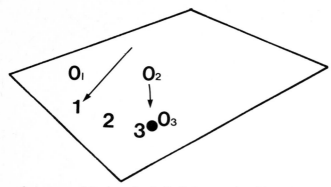

3 is now delaying the ball. 2 is covering him whilst 1 recovers to give depth and balance by restricting the freedom of 01. Consider for a moment the situation if 1 had not bothered to recover.

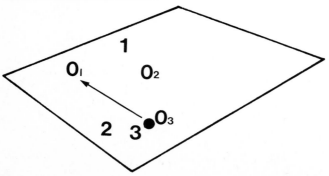

A pass from 03 to 01 would create a fine advantage to the attacking side.

So there is much to be gained in teaching players to think of themselves in all situations as either a 'Number 1, Number 2, or Number 3'.

They are 'Number 1' when the ball is played to the opponent nearest to them. Their job then is to pressurize by approaching on the correct angle to a position which forces the player on the ball to lower his head. The correct distance from the ball will be a point where with one foot anchored they can reach the ball with the other foot.

However many people play in the team, only one person can be Number 1 at any single time. So to 'Number 2'. Here the player nearest to 'Number 1' must give him cover. Again angle and distance are critical factors and must be learnt clearly.

All other players then become 'Number 3'. The job of these players is to provide balance and cover—the base of the defensive triangle. This can only be done (a) if they are on their goal side of the ball (b) if they mark opponents running past them, by running with them until danger is past.

Again it must be stressed that a single pass can change a player's function from being a '3' to a '1' and vice versa. This is the attraction of the game and in my experience using small-sided games in this way soon helps children understand basic tactics in a much more sensible way then talking about 4-2-4, 4-3-3 etc. etc. Sadly, so many fall into the trap of confusing young players by such talk, rather than enthusing them by sensible practice that is both instructive—and fun.

Attack

The same philosophy of being 1, 2 or 3 can be applied to attack, but first consider the jobs to be done.

First must come the player on the ball. He must know when to pass, shoot or dribble. He must recognize the situation presented by the positions of team mates and opponents. We must always encourage the development of individual skill and indeed, the practices earlier shown are intended to do just that. Yet we must also encourage an involvement in team play.

This can be done by encouraging all the other players to think in terms, first of helping the man on the ball. The question all must ask is 'Does he need help from me?'. If the answer is Yes, then the player must decide if he is at the right angle and distance to provide help.

For example. In Diagram 1 neither 02 nor 03 are in a good position to help 01.

But in Diagram 2 both players give him good support. Player 02 has changed his angle to give a passing chance forward whilst player 03 has changed both the angle and the distance of support. Player 1 may now elect:

    (a)   To dribble
    (b)   To pass to Player 02
    (c)   To pass to Player 03

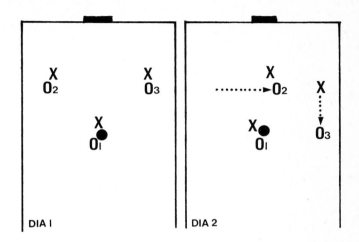

DIA 1   DIA 2

A full range of alternatives must create more problems for defenders. So providing support for the man on the ball must be a first priority.

Yet, we have to think in terms of going forward when support is established and so we build in our Player Number 3 theme again. In attack then, No 1 has the ball, No 2's provide support, No 3's are the players who are not needed for instant support. They can go forward.

Referring back to our Diagram 2 suppose 01 plays the ball to 02. 03 is already in a good supporting position as we see in Diagram 3.

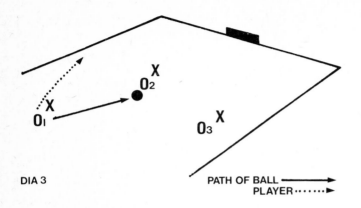

DIA 3

PATH OF BALL ——▶
PLAYER ·······▶

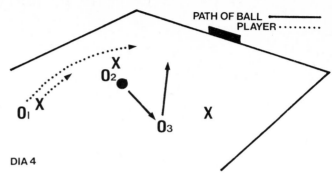

DIA 4

In other circumstances however, he may make a run to break down cover. See Diagram 5.

PATH OF BALL ——
PLAYER ········

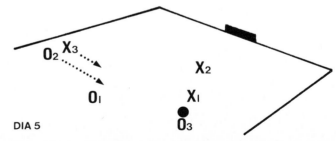

DIA 5

Player 01 can therefore go forward to threaten the back of the defence.

Two clear ways of going forward have been identified and these are as follows:-

1. To arrive un-noticed.
2. To break down defensive cover by taking players away from good positions.

In our example, player 01 wants to arrive un-noticed—so he will make a curved run round the back of defenders and can receive a pass from 03 in a shooting position after 03 has first received a pass from 02. See Diagram 4.

Here 01 provides support for 03 and notices 02 also coming across to support. Here we have support but no depth in front of the ball. 01 can give this depth and produce passing and dribbling chances for 03 by running in front of and past X2 as below in Diagram 6.

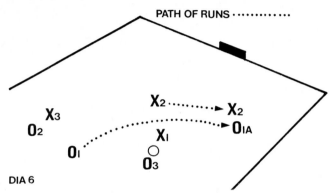

PATH OF RUNS ············

DIA 6

X2 has gone with 01 to 01A and X21 respectively, and cover has been broken. 03 can now dribble 1 v 1 against X1 or play to support 02 or pass forward to 01A and support the pass himself. The run of 01 made this possible by destroying the distance and angle of the defensive cover established by X2 and X1 in the first instance.

Thus these basic ground rules of play can be most effectively learnt and stressed in the small game form. Parents would do well to think of attacking and defending in terms of 1, 2, 3 and attempt to get their youngsters to learn the functions of each number no matter what the size of the game.

Summary

These are the thoughts and questions players must ask themselves as the game unfolds. Of course the first question is always 'What Number am I now?' In other words 'What to Do?' The following table give basic guide lines.

Defence

No 1 I must pressure the ball at the correct angle and distance.
No 2 I must cover No 1 at the correct angle and distance.
No 3 My job is to provide balance and cover. I must get back on our goal side of the ball first of all.

Attack

No 1 I have the ball. Do I have the chance to attack with it myself? Can I pass forward? If not I must content myself by retaining possession by playing to a support.
No 2 Does the player on the ball need my support? Am I at the right angle and distance to give it?
No 3 The player on the ball has full support. I can therefore go forward. Do I need to get behind defenders—or across and past them to destroy cover?

This may at first sight seem artificial and clumsy but in my experience using this technique and small sided games, even quite small boys learn the rudiments of team play and progress to doing things almost automatically. When this happens they have learnt to 'read the game'. Thus, just as when we learn to read a book we start with simple prose so in football we need smaller, uncluttered situations to help the learning process. A parent who can give time to watch and encourage boys to think on these lines in 3 v 3 games is doing a fine job and he (or she) can gain real satisfaction from watching the development of understanding grow in the play of the youngsters.

Small-sided games are the sign-posts to success. Even full-scale International matches can reduce to small-sided games. Here, the immediate game is 3 v 2 in an area approximately 20yds long by 10yds wide—just the sort of practice to provide fun—and learning in a garden or recreation area.

Pathways to success

Pathways to success

1. Children

Parents are usually keen to see their children develop skill and indeed this book is all about parents helping them so to do.

However, a word of warning. DO NOT PUSH TOO HARD. Football is a very big game and not merely a game played by 92 Football League Clubs. The worst thing that can happen from the point of view of both boy and game is to establish a feeling of rejection. The wise parent helps the boy to reach his best level of attainment—and enjoyment—within the structure of the game. There is no game quite like Association Football for allowing this to happen—and no game either where it is possible to kill all enthusiasm by passing on a feeling of lack of success.

It is not given to all to play soccer at professional level but as a game to enjoy and participate in fruitfully there is no substitute approaching the scale of opportunity which soccer represents.

We can look with this in mind, at the development of the child in the Pathways to Success.

a. Baby and infant stages

Encourage kicking and general playing with a ball. Large, colourful, plastic balls attract and excite children and are cheap and plentiful. They are also ideal to develop skill at this age. Make sure they are around the house and spend time in simple play with the child. He will dictate much of the activity by showing his interest—or lack of it—in the activity pursued. Remember the child is caught up in adjusting to himself and the whole situation of living—do not expect him to co-operate too much with others. Simple activities which help technique development are the key.

b. Junior stage

From the age of 7 to 9 or 10, the child experiences a growing involvement in, and awareness of others. This is the age of the 'gang' which carries over to as old as 13 or 14 in some cases. Use this to develop small games and activities based on soccer as well as the technique play referred to earlier. Here the boy may encounter organised team play at school for the first time. Encourage him by going to watch him but don't be too obtrusive. Don't make the mistake of exhorting him, and him alone, loudly from the touch line. Your presence and *quiet* encouragement are the greatest things here, allied to your willingness to talk over the game with him and taking time to go with him to watch good quality games afterwards.

c. Middle school

The years from 9—13 have been described as the 'Golden Years of Skill Learning'. Here the boy is sure to have the opportunity of playing and learning at school. Encourage as before. Continue to support the schoolmaster by your presence and by your activity at home. Here small sided games and technique go hand in hand. Where schemes exist for him to win badges for his involvement, work with him at practice to attain this. Above all teach him the right attitudes, both to co-operating with, and opposing others. It is here that attitudes firm up and young players should be encouraged to develop an attitude of give and take towards opponents and a good attitude towards both excellence and deficiencies in their own team mates—and themselves.

Again the right sort of parent—school link is vital. Where, as in many cases, the school is doing a fine job in assisting young players develop both skill and enthusiasm, the sound parent takes his lead from them as before. If no opportunities exist for play in school or school teams, it is here that a parent with groups of others can and do substitute themselves, by forming teams to give opportunities for play. Often teams of 5, 6, or 7-A-Side are formed and play in Recreational Department Play Scheme Competitions. This situation is excellent and should be encouraged.

d. Senior school
14—16 (or on to 19)

Here, the adolescent years, are often difficult times. Remember the boy is experiencing great emotional and physical change. Sympathetic parental help is needed—and a point of contact can be established through the game between parent and boy. By now the high flyer will be playing for School or even Town Schoolboys—parents of these boys may themselves feel rejected—but their support and encouragement is nevertheless still wanted.

Less successful players perhaps need help even more. This is especially the case for those boys who have no provision made for their competitive soccer in schools. Here, truly, is where neighbourhood teams of 11-A-Side can and should spring up to enable all those who wish to play to have the opportunity.

Remember however that it is right and proper that a boy's first loyalty should be to his school. It is where the school has not accepted its Association Football responsibility to boys that parents can make a contribution by forming teams to let them play.

As a schoolmaster, I encouraged parents to help in school matches. Under my direction, they helped referee, went away with teams and helped in so many ways. Not all schoolmasters, sadly, welcome such help. Nor, let it be said, are all parents keen enough to give it. However where good relations exist between parents and school, much good can come for the children by the fostering of them in these ways.

Parents of gifted boys may have an added problem—the possibility of a career in Professional Football. Care should be taken in assessing the boy's educational possibilities and liaison with school on this is vital. Many parents make the mistake of 'pushing' the boy into a career—not that most boys need much pushing. But the wise parent assesses the situation of the club and the provision it makes for continued education—as well as the provision it makes for the football development of the boy. Professional football, like theatre and music, is an honourable career, but it is as well to examine the pitfalls as well as the glamour before making a decision.

So it is that from the earliest to the last days of childhood, a parent can be a vital link in the development of his child's participation in the greatest game in the world.

Pathways to success

2. Parents

In the section on Children, I showed how I felt an involvement could be developed by parents. That involvement can be even greater if the parent, himself or herself, learns more about the game.

The Football Association runs excellent courses for those who wish to make such contributions.

It may be worthwhile to list some of the types of courses available:-

(a) *The Teaching Certificate*
Here is a course, available to all, WITHOUT EXAMINATION and with no bar on sex either! A course which deals with the basics of the game from the point of view of teaching and coaching and which also deals with the laws and the establishing of correct attitudes to play and competition. The Teaching Certificate of the Football Association is awarded upon completion. Details from Regional Coaches, County Coaching Secretaries or County Football Association Secretaries.

(b) *The Preliminary Coaching Award*
This award, for men only, helps develop a basic grounding in the principles of coaching. At preliminary level, examination is taken in (a) Practical Coaching (b) Practical Performance (c) Laws of the Game and (d) Theory of Coaching. Courses exist at local, regional and national level and full details can be obtained from County Coaching Secretaries or the Regional Coaches of the Football Association. A Qualifying Award is also available for those who succeed here to attempt at national level only.

(c) *Referees*
The County Football Associations, through their Referees section also run excellent courses to qualify those who wish to contribute in this way. Courses are usually available at local centres and the County Football Association Secretaries will supply full details.

(d) *Treatment of Injury*

Again the Football Association runs fine courses at local, regional and national levels in this important area. Details from Regional Coaches or County Football Associations.

(e) *Administration*

County Football Assocations from time to time organise courses to deal with club administration and all that it entails. Obviously therefore, details from County Football Association Secretaries.

Here then is an established structure which is available to all who wish to improve their knowledge. Add to this the work of the Coaches Associations and their counter-parts in the vital world of Refereeing and it becomes clear that all who wish to make a contribution can find capable aid close at hand.

Again, it is not given to all to be associated at professional level. Yet to the game, all clubs from the highest to the most humble are of importance. Strength in depth is soccer's greatest card—an strength like this comes only from commitment and involvement across the board. In this respect who can play a more vital part than the interested and informed parent?

Forming a club

Forming a club

Practice—however enjoyable—is only really worthwhile if it leads to a real end—playing a game. So it is natural that parents and friends of young players sooner or later look to forming a club to play games against other teams.

In the introductory section of this book mention was made regarding the advisability of games of less than 11-A-Side for young players. Often now Recreation Departments will run Leagues for 5-A-Side and even 7-A-Side involvement and it is recommended that those dealing with young players explore these possibilities to the full.

However, there is always a right and a wrong way to set about any task—and forming and running a club, however small, is no exception. Let's look at the correct procedure.

Organisation of football

Association Football in this Country is governed by the Football Association which delegates responsibility to the County Football Associations who cover the Country. The County Football Associations, through their Secretary, will be the biggest source of help and encouragement to those wishing to form and run clubs at all levels of the game. Any queries or problems should be put to them BEFORE taking action—and their advice implemented. They know all the problems and pitfalls and have the experience which many wishing to form teams will lack.

Steps to take

An experienced County Secretary has suggested these steps towards forming a Club, and it will be seen that they are simple and logical and designed to help rather than hinder.

1. Establish that there are sufficient players interested.
2. Call a meeting of potential Officers. These will be mature people able and willing to take on the administrative tasks involved. Elect and appoint Officers—(a) Chairman, (b) Secretary, (c) Treasurer (d) Committee. It is desirable that the posts of Secretary and Treasurer are held by two people, although it is accepted that in practice this is not always possible.
3. Acquire access to a pitch. This is often easier to say than do—especially in urban areas. Here, the Recreation Department at the Town Hall will be able to indicate the possibility of hiring a municipal pitch. Generally this will be easier to do on Saturdays and Sundays but a word of caution, for boys still at school, it must be remembered that schools have first loyalty call. The English Schools Football Association, through its district organisations organises much excellent competition for boys and a wise parent encourages his boy to play in school football above all. In more rural areas, there are still a few farmers and landowners who may be prepared to allow a field to be used for playing purposes, but it must be stated

that provision for playing pitches is generally a difficult problem. Parents forming clubs should recognize this as a stiff hurdle—but there is one consolation. If there are not pitches available, then there must be many teams in the area—teams which could use any help you might be able to offer and who could provide competition for your child if there is no provision for him in the school system.

4. Open the necessary books. These are as follows:-
   (a) A Cash Account Book.
   (b) A Register of Players.
   (c) A Minute Book for Meetings.
5. Apply to the County Football Association for AFFILIATION. Only affiliated clubs are allowed to play in recognised competitions. The County Football Association will send a simple Affiliation Form for completion. If you have followed the previous steps then this form will present no problems.
6. After affiliation apply for membership of the competition of your choice—again the County Football Association will be able to assist you with any queries regarding who to contact.
7. Raise your funds. Again, often easier to say than to do but by combining subscriptions, competitions and fund raising events, wonders can be—and are—achieved.
8. Start playing.

Qualities and activities of officials

1. The Chairman

The Chairman of a Club is usually a mature person of some local standing. It is desirable that the Chairman is more than a figure head for it is he who has the ultimate responsibility for club affairs. Often, he will be the sheet anchor in providing finance or facilities, but this should not be his sole quality. Involvement is the key. The post of President could be the niche for a benevolent finance-giving friend. The post of Chairman requires a well balanced enthusiast who, above all, has a love of football and the well being of young players at heart.

2. The Secretary

It is often said 'Find a good Secretary and you will find a good club'. This is certainly true. The Secretary is the lynch-pin of the club. He, above all, must be enthusiastic, efficient and be prepared to devote time to the various tasks. He will be responsible for communications to Leagues, County Football Association, players etc. Often he will take on responsibility for seeing the pitch is marked out, the referees looked after, liaising with opponents and ensuring equipment is organised properly. In short, he must be either a jack of all trades or a sensible delegator, passing on tasks to other Committee members (or players) who he knows can carry them out successfully. The running of the club day to day, week to week, stands or falls by his efforts. Often he will take on the added tasks of coach, guide, philosopher and friend to all. In short, he will, certainly without pay, and often apparently without thanks, be the one man to provide the firm base a successful club needs.

3. The Treasurer

Obviously the Treasurer must be someone who can keep simple accounts efficiently and someone who can be a real right hand man to the Secretary. Whilst the financial running of a club is a vital task in its own right, the Treasurer can be a great asset in several other directions. From the list of activities related under the post of Secretary, it will be seen that the tasks involved in running a club are many and various—a good treasurer will certainly be able to undertake some of these burdens in addition to his normal Treasurer's responsibilities.

4. The Committee

Where possible other interested adults may be persuaded to join a Committee.

It is perhaps fair to say that most Committees are not as efficient as they might be because those serving on them are not given specific tasks. It is suggested that each individual be given a specific task or tasks (according to size of Committee). Thus, with each person having a task or responsibility and reporting to regular meetings of the Officers, action is more probable.

Examples of some of the responsibilities which might be allocated are as follows:-

(a) Equipment, provision, maintainence, and possibly even laundry. This does not necessarily mean that the person responsible will necessarily physically wash the shirts himself, but will devise and ensure the running of the policy to be adopted by the club.

(b) Pitch. The pitch may require marking, nets erecting and storing etc. As a boy my greatest disappointment was to turn up to play on a pitch with poor markings and no nets—maybe that may sound too sophisticated—but we live even more today, in a sophisticated age. Again the Committee person may merely organise a rota of players to perform the tasks. If he ensures it is carried through successfully, he is worth his weight in gold!

(c) Finance Raising. Any Treasurer would be glad to have the support of a member prepared to organise such tasks.

(d) Team Management. Acquiring the help of someone who can help in this area should not be neglected. Someone with an F.A. Coaching Qualification is desirable, but often someone looking to gain such qualification will take on the task to gain the necessary experience he needs to be successful. Again the County Football Association or local Coaches Association may be able to offer advice and suggestions. Of course the best thing is for someone within the local structure to take on the task and then himself go on one of the many local Coaching Courses run by the Football Association.

(e) Treatment of Injury. All clubs should have at the very least a basic first aid kit and someone who can use it sensibly.

Conclusion

Running a club is not necessarily difficult, although bad planning can make it so. It does however require TIME and ENTHUSIASM above all. Properly organised many hands can make light work. In this connection, it should be recorded that much excellent work in club administration can, and is, done by WOMEN. MUMS as well as DADS have a contribution to make. Family involvement in soccer is something to be encouraged and ladies often make light of important tasks that defeat mere males!

There are 37,500 or more clubs affiliated to the Football Association which give a lot of pleasure, not only to the young boys and men who play in them and a lot of satisfaction (and no doubt some frustration also) to the dedicated armies of club officials who administer them.

Perhaps the question can now be asked 'Could you form a Club'? If you cannot form a club yourself then perhaps you have something to offer to an existing club—football and young people need someone like you—people who are prepared to 'Teach Your Child' (and the children of others) to play the greatest game in the world. The Football Association, 16 Lancaster Gate, London W.2. will be able to give you the name of your local County Football Association, Regional Coach and Coaches Association who will be able to supply you with your local points of contact.